Brothers Wreck

Jada Alberts

CURRENCY PRESS
The performing arts publisher

CURRENCY PLAYS

First published in 2014
by Currency Press Pty Ltd,
Suite 310, 46-56 Kippax Street, Surry Hills, NSW 2010, Australia
enquiries@currency.com.au
www.currency.com.au

in association with Belvoir

Reprinted 2016, 2020, 2024.

Cataloguing-in-Publication data for this title is available from the National Library of Australia.

Typeset by Dean Nottle for Currency Press.
Cover design by Alphabet Studio.

Currency Press acknowledges the Traditional Owners of the Country on which we live and work. We pay our respects to all Aboriginal and Torres Strait Islander Elders, past and present.

Contents

for Teina, Temeka,
Rokiah, Taituha,
Jarrod, James and Slade

Weight, weight, O heavy weight,
This stormy night I meet my fate,
A squall, a wall, a sky of water,
A minute more till heaven's gates.

And there amongst this troubled sea,
My brother's hand stretched out for me.

Could I be some use to you?
This little boat tossed through and through.

Still tie me to my brother's bow,
This night will end, I know not how.

Book of Sorrows Black
Jada Alberts

Brothers Wreck was first produced by Belvoir at Belvoir St Theatre, Sydney, on 28 May 2014, with the following cast:

DAVID	Cramer Cain
PETRA	Lisa Flanagan
ADELE	Rarriwuy Hick
RUBEN	Hunter Page-Lochard
JARROD	Bjorn Stewart

Director, Leah Purcell
Set and Costume Designer, Dale Ferguson
Lighting Designer, Luiz Pampolha
Composer and Sound Designer, Brendan O'Brien
Stage Manager, Luke McGettigan
Assistant Stage Manager, Keiren Smith

CHARACTERS

RUBEN, early 20s, seemingly untouchable, Ruben is impulsive, quick-witted and sometimes aggressive. He thinks he's figured out the world and his place in it. Ruben's mum died when he was young so he was raised by one of his aunties, Adele's mum.

ADELE, mid 20s, Ruben's cousin and sister. Adele is dedicated, sure of herself, mostly calm and always loyal. She has a tendency to worry.

JARROD, mid 20s, Adele's boyfriend. He's cheeky, thoughtful and quietly confident. Good with his hands, Jarrod loves to make or fix things, mostly engines.

DAVID, late 30s, Ruben's counsellor. David is a former teacher who has worked in the Darwin area most of his life.

PETRA, 40s, the youngest of three sisters, Petra is Adele and Ruben's aunty.

SETTING

A space of a Darwin home—we can't tell if its indoors or outdoors. Possibly under a house on stilts, maybe a big verandah. Somewhere, there is a door that leads somewhere else—it has both a screen door and a solid door behind it. Next to the screen door is a window, open louvres.

There's a table and chairs to sit at and a kitchenette somewhere, a place to make cups of tea and a sink. A ceiling fan spins slowly.

NOTES

The first scene takes place six months earlier than the present.

A forward slash (/) indicates overlapping dialogue.

This play went to press before the end of rehearsals and may differ from the play as performed.

SCENE ONE

Six months ago. Dawn. August, during the build-up.

RUBEN *is sitting in the hallway, against a wall.* ADELE *enters, dressed in basketball shorts and a singlet. She's just woken up. She sees* RUBEN.

ADELE: You're up early.

> *She crosses to the table and takes a cigarette and lighter from a packet. She puts the cigarette in her mouth but doesn't light it. She goes to the kitchen and boils the kettle.*

Jesus, this heat is killin me.

> *She waits for the kettle to boil, makes a tea. Milky, two sugars.*

You slept?

> *She heads outside with her tea and cigarette.*

Why you sittin there, weirdo?

> *As* ADELE *exits,* RUBEN *attempts to say something to her, nothing comes out.* ADELE *gets outside and we hear her mug hit the ground. She stumbles back inside, shocked, stunned.*

Joe! Jarrod, Jarrod, Jarrod! Jarrooood!
JARROD: [*offstage*] Whaaat?
ADELE: Joe, he's… hurry! Hurry!

> ADELE *looks at* RUBEN.

JARROD: [*offstage*] What?
ADELE: Jarroood!
JARROD: [*offstage*] I'm up, what?!

> JARROD *enters.*

ADELE: Hurry—

> ADELE *rushes outside,* JARROD *follows behind her.*

JARROD: What's going /
ADELE: Help me lift him—
JARROD: No, no, no, Joe—
ADELE: Get a knife. [*Beat.*] Knife, Jarrod!

JARROD enters running. He goes to the kitchen, grabs a large knife and runs back outside.

Hurry!

We hear a plastic chair dragged, repositioned. JARROD *stands on it and tries to cut his friend Joe out of a makeshift noose.*

JARROD: It's not working. Fuck… the sinkers—
ADELE: I can't hold him—
JARROD: Knife's blunt… [*He drops the knife.*] Fuck!
ADELE: [*calling to* RUBEN] Ruben?! Grab another knife!

JARROD runs in, grabs another knife, runs out again.

I can't hold / him!
JARROD: I've got him, I've got him!

They swap position. We hear JARROD *lift Joe's body.* ADELE *stands on the plastic chair. Sounds of a knife cutting through net.*

Hurry, Del.
ADELE: It's not cutting!
JARROD: Ruben!
ADELE: Fuuuuck!
JARROD: Can you untie it?
ADELE: I don't know.
JARROD: Try.

Beat.

ADELE: My hands.
JARROD: You can do it.
ADELE: It's tangled.
JARROD: Give it a sec.
ADELE: I'm making it worse. Fuck!

The second knife drops to the ground.

Oh my God, I can't…

ADELE *is crying.*

JARROD: Ruben! [*To* ADELE] Oi, it's okay—
ADELE: It's not fucking okay—
JARROD: / Ruben!

ADELE: I gotta get down—
JARROD: Lift him, / I'll try—
ADELE: [*sobbing*] Get him down, Jarrod, get him down —
JARROD: RUBEN!
ADELE: Get him down, get him down—

> JARROD *walks into the house and looks at* RUBEN.

[*Crying*] God… Jooooe!

> RUBEN *'s broken in the corner, hiding his head.* JARROD *leaves him, goes back outside.*

JARROD: Come inside, Del.
ADELE: No, no, I won't—
JARROD: Come inside, / bub, now.
ADELE: No, no—
JARROD: There's nothing / we can do—
ADELE: Get him down, Jarrod, get him… Put me down, arsehole!

> JARROD *enters carrying* ADELE *over his shoulder.*

JARROD: Stop, Del—
ADELE: Put me down!

> JARROD *puts* ADELE *down, stands in her way, blocking her.*

JARROD: There's nothing we can do—
ADELE: I won't leave him out there alone.
JARROD: He's gone, bub.
ADELE: I'm not leaving him!

> ADELE *tries to get past* JARROD. *He holds her, restrains her, but she manages to make ground towards the door.*

JARROD: Ruben—
ADELE: Move, / don't leave him—
JARROD: Shut the door!
ADELE: Joey! / Joe!
JARROD: / Ruben!

> RUBEN *stands.*

ADELE: Fucking / move!
JARROD: Shut the door, Ruben!
ADELE: Let me / go!

RUBEN *rushes towards the door.*

JARROD: Ruben, SHUT THE FUCKING DOOR!

RUBEN *finally slams the door shut.*

SCENE TWO

Six months later. It's April, the beginning of the dry season.

RUBEN *sits outside his old house, Balnba Road, iPod on, white earpieces in his ears. We hear the track as he would: 'Rule the World' by Jimblah. He stands under a street lamp looking at the old house. He has a cap on backwards and a can of Southern Comfort in one hand, a cigarette in the other.*

RUBEN *mumbles a chorus to himself then takes one earpiece out. As he sings he takes a full can of Southern Comfort.*

RUBEN: Brother.

He opens it, pours it on the ground.

SCENE THREE

RUBEN *in David's office. Counselling session nine.* DAVID *is holding a document, a copy of Ruben's statement to police taken the morning Joe died.*

RUBEN: I don't live there no more.

DAVID: I'm just reading what it says.

RUBEN: Yeah, well it's wrong.

DAVID: It's where it happened, Ruben, that's why it's in here.

RUBEN: Don't make it less wrong, I don't live there. It's not my address.

DAVID: Alright, I got it. Not your address. [*Pause.*] Balnba Road. That's a Larrakia word, isn't it? What's it mean?

RUBEN: You askin the wrong blackfella. [*Beat.*] Don't you mob believe in air con?

DAVID: Ants got to the wiring. You want a glass of water?

RUBEN: Whole of Darwin's on flood watch, mate, I don't need water.

DAVID: Can't handle the heat? [*Pause.*] So your statement then. [*Beat.*] It's your ninth session. I don't wanna push you, mate, but we have to

/ talk about what happened with—

RUBEN: Go on then, read it out loud.

DAVID: If you don't want me to read it, I won't read it.

RUBEN: Whatever, dude, you do whatever, talk whatever you wanna talk.

Pause.

DAVID: This gonna play out like the first eight?

RUBEN: Had a pretty shitty day, who know's, maybe you're in for a show.

DAVID: So let's do tomorrow instead then. Morning or afternoon?

RUBEN: You've bored me shitless enough today, no way I'm comin back tomorrow to start again.

Silence.

'I don't wanna push ya, mate.' Yes ya bloody do. [*Beat.*] Big hero, aren't ya? Helpin out the slum dogs.

DAVID: Slum dogs?

RUBEN: Palmerston. Everyone's some kinda dog out there. Got the sly dogs, the copper dogs, mad dogs, the stray dogs, the slum dogs, every kinda dog you can think of. I'm surprised you haven't been out there, picked yourself up a pup.

DAVID: And you reckon I talk shit?

Pause.

RUBEN: So we talk then, no more bullshit.

DAVID: Fine with me.

Beat.

RUBEN: So where you live? Where'd you grow up? Wait, let me guess, Callum Bay.

DAVID: Stuart Park.

RUBEN: I can see that. I can see that. So, what, private school then? [*Beat.*] Don't be shame. You get born into some nice little cosy-arse family, they gonna send you off to Sacred Heart or Saint whoever—don't be shame, good for you, Stuart Park.

DAVID: You don't know what you're talkin about.

RUBEN: You had choices, that's all I'm sayin. You never had to slum it. [*Beat.*] We used to have these shitty old books about space. The universe and whatever. Mum'd read 'em just before bed. I'd have these weird-arse cartoon dreams where I'd bounce around on fluffy white clouds, take a trip to Mars, go anywhere. Be whatever. Poor little black boy from the arse-end of the earth, dreamin like he's white and rich. It's bullshit, of course, but no-one tells ya that, do they? They don't tell you shit till you're 15 and then it's, 'Why haven't you got a job yet, why haven't you made somethin of yourself, why you so friggin lazy, Ruben, where have ya been? You wanna stick to something for once, Ruben, you better sort yourself out, boy, 'cause rent don't pay for itself.' [*Beat.*] How many jobs you had, Stuart Park?

DAVID: My name's David.

RUBEN: Count yourself lucky you got the suburb, bro, where I come from you're only ever as good as the street you live on. How many jobs?

DAVID: A few.

RUBEN: Well, jobs aren't shit, really, are they? I mean unless you're a theoretical physicist, a cosmologist… Kanye. [*Beat.*] Not really jobs but, ay? 'Cause I've had jobs. Mad Harry's. Was boring as hell, didn't rock up, got fired. Worked on the mines for a bit, was rollin in it. Bought a car with the moneys.

One of my uncles going off every time I saw him, 'You've sold your soul to the devil, boy!' Says ya can't be a black man and work for the dogs rippin up your homelands. Mum says, 'Don't worry 'bout him, he'll be after a loan next week'. [*Beat.*] Money's a hassle, not worth it. More money you got, more you lose.

DAVID: Maybe you haven't found the right one yet. Good job should be something you enjoy doing, something you care about.

RUBEN: That why you do it, 'cause you care? [*Beat.*] My sister says you used to be Mr Stuart Park.

DAVID: I was, yeah.

RUBEN: You don't teach anymore but?

DAVID: No.

RUBEN: Why not? [*Pause.*] It's cool. I already know.

DAVID: Not here to talk about me.

RUBEN: Fair enough. [*Beat.*] Taste of your own medicine right there, huh. [*Beat.*] Well, while you're care-ing your way across Darwin, Mother Teresa, rest of the world just wants to make a quick buck. It don't take an astronaut to figure that one out. Bugger it, I say. Rather be poor, hang out with my family.

Beat.

DAVID: You don't get bored?

RUBEN: Shit no, there's plenty to do round here. Go fishing, hunt down parts for the *Front Yard Challenge*. Wish someone would've paid me to do that, I was good at that. Sometimes I come round to thinkin 'bout gettin another job. Nah, fuck it! Back in line at Centrelink, spend up big on my basics card. I sleep too much, don't sleep enough, drive around, spend *whole days* just drivin people round. Settin traps at low tide, skint till payday, couldn't care less. Iced coffee for breakfast, chillin out mostly, Xbox, Southern Comfort for lunch, bummin smokes, drivin bush, fishtails on Dick Ward Drive, firecrackers at three in the mornin, holy shit, Jah, this is Darwin, man, it's the fuckin life!

> RUBEN *laughs at himself, gets his rollies out from his pocket and begins to roll.*

DAVID: What's the 'front yard challenge'?

RUBEN: Tinny. Little four-man boat us boys found.

> RUBEN *lights his cigarette.*

DAVID: I'd prefer if you didn't smoke in here.

> RUBEN *exhales smoke towards* DAVID.

Brother, you can't smoke in here.

> DAVID *takes the cigarette from* RUBEN*'s mouth. He stubs the lit end on a piece of paper trying to put it out.*

RUBEN: Oi, they don't grow on trees, you know.

DAVID: Actually, they do. What about your dad? Let's talk about him, sounds like he's had an interesting life.

RUBEN: What, from his criminal record? I wouldn't bloody know, I'm just his kid. Stop squashing that smoke, would ya? Give it back.

> DAVID *hands back the extinguished cigarette.*

Been doing some research, have we?

DAVID: It's my job.

RUBEN: Well, you're barkin up the wrong tree, Nancy Drew, that bloke don't mean shit to me. Yeah, he knows how to make an appearance when it suits him, drop by like he never left. I'll never forget seein' the

bloke at Mum's funeral, dressed in a flash suit. I was seven but I remember. 'Wow, that's my dad, he looks like a nice bloke. He's gonna
look after me now, 'cause that's what dads do.' I was a delusional little
bugger, I'll give ya that. [*Beat.*] I don't want nuthin to do with him. He
doesn't give a shit, why should I? I can count on one hand how many
times that bloke's asked me a question.

DAVID: How many times is that?

> *Beat.*

RUBEN: [*smiling*] Oo… smooth. Hit a sore spot. You can have that round.

DAVID: It's not a game, Ruben.

RUBEN: Oh come on, I'm givin you that one, take it. So what have we
covered so far? Got the Dad issues, check. Mum passed away, check.
Aunty had to raise me, check. No / father figure…

DAVID: Ruben—

RUBEN: Shit, I'm gonna break down! But that's alright 'cause you can fix
me, ay, tell me everything's gonna be / alright.

DAVID: That's enough, mate,

RUBEN: [*laughing*] What? Isn't this what you want? You want me to talk
and I'm talking! This is all the bad shit, Mr Stuart Park. Help me, Mr
Stuart Park, please, you're my only hope! That what you wanna hear?

DAVID: That's a lot of bullshit for someone who just agreed to cut the
bullshit. [*Beat.*] You finished?

RUBEN: Yeah. I think I am.

DAVID: Why'd you hit the copper? [*Pause.*] Why'd you hit the copper,
Ruben? [*Pause.*] Did he say something about Joe?

RUBEN: Time's up, I reckon.

DAVID: No, it's not.

RUBEN: I gotta roll, brother, we can save this poxy conversation for another time. Catch ya later, Stuart Park.

> RUBEN *exits.*

SCENE FOUR

Outside the Beach Front Hotel.

RUBEN *is smashed, drunk off his head. He holds a can of Southern Comfort in his hands.* JARROD *is with him, on his phone. He's trying to make*

a call.

RUBEN: [*yelling across the road*] Let's find out then, ay!… Call the pigs!
… I don't care, idiot, call 'em!… Do it, call 'em! I'll crack you all!
JARROD: Shut up.

RUBEN *stops yelling.*

RUBEN: I'm not scared. That bouncer's an idiot. [*Beat. Yelling again*]
Hear that, mung bean? You're an idiot!… Bring it, cheese boy!
JARROD: Shut up, Rue!

His call isn't going through. He keeps trying. RUBEN *has a massive smile on his face, he is in his element.*

RUBEN: Piece of… Ay, look! A break in the rain!
JARROD: Oi, sit down, before they call the cops for real.

JARROD *tries to call again.*

RUBEN: Let 'em come.
JARROD: So much for takin it easy.
RUBEN: I'll fight 'em, crack 'em all.

He searches around for a smoke, notices JARROD *on the phone.*

Who ya callin?

JARROD *doesn't respond, he's looking at his phone.*

Oi, dickhead, who ya callin?
JARROD: Watch your mouth, idiot. I'm callin your sister, get your dumb
arse outta here.
RUBEN: Alright, alright. Ra-lax. Sheesh.
JARROD: I was relaxed, till you got us kicked out of the friggin bar. I hope
you're happy.

RUBEN *smiles big and sits on the ground against the wall, having
found a cigarette. He lights it.*

RUBEN: Ay, ay. 'Member when we seen that cop car at them lights just
there, all us mob? [*Beat.*] Car was full up, unlicensed, unregistered,
Aunty yelling from the front seat, 'Duck down, Duck down!'
JARROD: You're drunk
RUBEN: Cop car right behind us, cramp in my neck tryin to hide, then,
nek minut we hear it, blaring from the paddy wagon, [*rapping*]

'Fuck the police, fuck the police, fuck the police!'

JARROD: Uncle Adam… mad crack.

RUBEN: [*laughing*] Blaring 'fuck the police' from his own bloody paddy wagon, funny bastard. What a crack-up. You 'member that?

JARROD: Yeah, I remember. Us boys were celebrating, we'd finally got her to float. The *Front Yard Challenge*. Joey's skinny arse nearly got stuck under the console. Had to bust the glove box to get him out.

RUBEN: Ha. Yeah.

> *Beat.*

JARROD: You go to counselling today?

RUBEN: I forgot that bit.

JARROD: Did you go, drongo?

> RUBEN *puts out his smoke and pats down his pockets looking for more. Finds a packet, it's empty. He scrunches it up, throws it.*

RUBEN: Yes, stickybeak, I went. You got any smokes?

JARROD: I quit, remember? Two weeks I haven't had one.

RUBEN: What? What for? Ay, rollies.

> RUBEN *starts searching his pockets again.*

JARROD: What do you mean, what for?

RUBEN: Wait first.

> *Having found his rollies,* RUBEN *halts the conversation to focus on rolling a cigarette.*

> JARROD *redials a number on his phone.*

On payday they all look at me funny when I ask for two soft packs and a 30-gram pouch, but who's laughin now? So as I never. Run. Out.

JARROD: Well done, Rue, outsmarted the lot of us. Shame you can't get on the charge without startin on randoms.

RUBEN: [*lighting his smoke*] What? I don't.

JARROD: Yes you do.

RUBEN: When else have I?

JARROD: Yesterday, dickhead.

RUBEN: Oh yeah.

> RUBEN *laughs.*

JARROD: You're lucky the cops aren't here already.

RUBEN: See, that's the problem with you, Jarrod, you're soft. Not me, I'll break any bloke's neck, I won't hesitate.

JARROD *redials while he's talking. He's heard all this before.*

JARROD: You wanna watch your mouth, callin me soft.

RUBEN: There we go, there it is.

JARROD: Shuddup. Del don't care what that bloke in there did to her, why should you?

RUBEN: No-one messes with my sister, not him, not any bloke. So much as a hair on that girl's head gets outta place, I'll kill a cunt, I don't give a shit. I'm not soft like you, Jarrod, I go all-out.

JARROD'*s phone call is answered. He speaks to* ADELE *on the other line.*

JARROD: Del… Where are ya?… Yeah, I got him… Yeah… I'll tell ya later… What's wrong?… Nah, it's right, we can walk, bub.

RUBEN *looks at him.*

We can walk… [*Beat.*] Only if you don't mind… Alright… Okay, bub … Yep, love you. 'Bye.

JARROD *hangs up the phone, puts it in his pocket.*

RUBEN: We can walk? You didn't tell her we're walkin, did ya?

JARROD: She's comin, she's gonna be a while.

RUBEN: Why, where is she?

JARROD: She's gotta take Izzy to the hospital, her legs.

RUBEN: Again? Jezuus… Getting old is fucked. [*He burps loudly. Fondly*] My mother. Isabella Maria. Aunty Izzy wizzy, always bizzy… Ay, you wanna sneak round the back, jump the fence? I got one more 20, my shout.

JARROD: You wouldn't make it over the fence.

RUBEN: What? Yeah, I could.

JARROD: If that bouncer sees you anywhere near the place, you'll be in the back of a paddy wagon before you can shit. Let's just wait for Del.

RUBEN: Pansy. See? You soft, bro! Carn, be a man, take a risk! What you scared of, Jarrod? You scared of the itty bitty po-lice. [*He yells.*] Fuck that little bitch of a bouncer! Fuuuucck him up his whhite—!

JARROD *grabs him. Slams him against the wall.*

JARROD: Shut the fuck up. You feel like getting locked up, ay? Ay?

> JARROD *lets* RUBEN *go and walks away.*

RUBEN: Yeah, maybe I do! [*Beat. Ferociously*] Fuck you.

JARROD: Yeah, off ya go.

> *Silence.*

RUBEN: I'll sit down then, will I? I'll wait… Pansy Jarrod wants me to wait? So I'll wait.

> *Beat.*

JARROD: Good.

RUBEN: Good.

JARROD: Del'll be here soon.

RUBEN: Good. Great. I'll wait with you then, brother.

> *Pause.*

> RUBEN *can't sit still for long. He gets to his feet and paces.*

She's a good woman, my sister, isn't she?

JARROD: What?

RUBEN: My sister, deafhead.

JARROD: Just relax, Ruben.

RUBEN: Nah, I'm saying she's good, aren't I, I'm sayin she's good to ya.

JARROD: Yeah, alright, she's good to me.

RUBEN: That's all I'm saying, she's good. She's good to / you…

JARROD: Of course she's / good to me.

RUBEN: And she's good to me too, don't matter that we're cousins, we grew up together. Brother and sister, same blood, her mother is my mother.

JARROD: She's your sister, I know that. Youse are family.

RUBEN: Yeah, we are. And I'll protect her till the day I die. And that maggot in there, *any* maggot that fucks her round, I don't give a shit if he's family, or not.

> JARROD *starts laughing.*

No matter *who* he is—

JARROD: Shit, man, what you gonna do? What?

RUBEN: What?

JARROD: Nah, keep goin, brus, don't let me interrupt.

RUBEN: Nah, what? Why you being a smart-arse?

JARROD: That dude woulda ripped you apart in there!

RUBEN: Whatever, you don't know / shit.

JARROD: He's twice your size, dickhead! And why the hell you lookin at me sideways for, you gonna bash me too? Come on then, Rambo! [*Beat.*] You know she sent me down here, don't ya?

RUBEN: So. So what?

JARROD: Wherever you got this, this dickhead prancing around thing, thinkin it's your job to protect everyone, piss it off, man, makes you look real stupid, Rubes. Seriously. Especially seein as you can't even look after yourself. [*Beat.*] She sent me to get you, Rue. Who's lookin after who, here?

RUBEN: What the fuck are you saying? Stop talkin in riddles, man, I'm charged.

JARROD: I know that, brother, I know.

RUBEN: I'll kill anyone who hurts my family. Kill 'em. [*Beat.*] That's what I'm saying.

JARROD: That's pretty clear, brother, I get it. I just mean, there's no need to be so aggro about it. Del doesn't need you runnnin around smashin blokes 'cause they stole her lunch money in primary school. Your sister's a rock.

RUBEN: Yeah well, I'll take on any bloke, I don't give a shit. That's who I am, it's what I'm good at. Anyone wanna mess with us, they can answer to me.

JARROD: Alright, hero. Alright.

RUBEN: I don't know why you gotta talk to me like this when I'm drunk, man, buzz kill.

> RUBEN *is stumbling around, looking like he could fall over at any minute.*

JARROD: Rubes, because… [*Beat.*] Alright, man. I'll stop. I'll stop if you sit down.

RUBEN: Fine.

> *He attempts to sit but sort of falls to the ground.*

[*Laughing*] Ayy, the ground moved. I'm alright. I'm alright. [*Pause.*] Got a smoke, bro?

SCENE FIVE

Midnight.

RUBEN *and* JARROD *sit amongst pillows and blankets watching a TV turned up very loud. Underneath the sound of the TV is a frog-croaking orchestra.*

ADELE *enters the room and throws her bag on the table, leans on the back of a chair. Till the TV is turned off, everybody yells.*

ADELE: It's a bit loud, don't you think?
JARROD: What?
ADELE: I said it's a bit loud!
JARROD: Rue, turn it down.
RUBEN: What?
JARROD: Turn it down, bro.
RUBEN: Why?
JARROD: Just do it.
ADELE: Jesus.
RUBEN: I don't have the remote.
JARROD: You had it there.
RUBEN: Well, I don't have it now.
JARROD: Where'd you put it?

> RUBEN *and* JARROD *are pulling up blankets, looking under pillows.*

RUBEN: I don't know where it is!
ADELE: Fuuuck.
JARROD: We're lookin, Del.
RUBEN: Maybe it's in the kitchen?
JARROD: Just find it, dude.
RUBEN: I'm looking, I'm looking.

> *He rushes to the kitchen.* ADELE *pulls a power cord from the wall. The TV is silenced. The sound of the frog orchestra is very apparent now.*

Oh, you found it.
JARROD: Sort of.
RUBEN: The frogs are too loud, Del, I couldn't hear Marky Mark.
ADELE: You wanna shut them frogs up, Jarrod!

JARROD: How?

ADELE: I don't fuckin care *how*, just…

> *She grabs a broom that's close by, bangs it on the walls and beams that are closest, yelling at the frogs to be quiet.*

SHUT UP, YOU FAT GREEN BASTARDS!

> *The frogs fall silent.*

JARROD: Jesus, Del… what's goin on?

ADELE: You wanna clear all the water from the yard, mate! You wanna empty them pot plants! I asked you to do it days ago after the last rain. I won't have them keepin me up at night, you hear me? Get rid of the water!

JARROD: Alright!

> ADELE *lazily chucks the broom, exhausted by her sudden outburst.*
>
> *Silence.*

RUBEN: Mum still in the car?

> *Silence.*

JARROD: Del… [*Beat.*] Where's your mum?

ADELE: Doctor said it was best she stay. She's there. At the hospital.

RUBEN: Her knee get worse?

> *Silence.*

ADELE: They drained her knee, gave her morphine. [*Beat.*] The doctor… he had a feel of Mum's stomach, just to check. [*Beat.*] He… he found a lump, a big lump on her right side, near her rib cage. He said it was probably nuthin. Just wanted to check. [*Beat.*] We waited for an ultrasound. She got tired. [*Beat.*] Then he said it. The ultrasound must of… There's a tumour on her liver. [*Beat.*] I guess it looks bad. He wouldn't let me bring her home.

> *Silence.*
>
> RUBEN *gets up, crosses the room to pick up his cigarettes…*

Ruben.

RUBEN: She'll be alright… She'll be right. I know it. [*Beat.*] I'm just gonna… I'll be back.

> *Picking up his lighter,* RUBEN *exits.*

As he leaves a steady, gentle rain starts to fall.

ADELE: More rain.

A frog starts to croak, quickly joined by a few more.

JARROD: I'll empty the pots.

> JARROD *stands to leave.*

ADELE: Don't leave, Jay. Fuck the frogs... Don't leave.

> JARROD *goes to* ADELE *who's still sitting. He holds her head against him as the rain and the frogs get louder.*

SCENE SIX

RUBEN *is back in David's office for another counselling session.*

RUBEN: Can't stay long today, got somewhere to be.

DAVID: You know the drill, Ruben, court says you have to be here for the duration of the hour or I can't sign off on it. If you need to leave we can reschedule?

RUBEN: Can't even give us a break, can ya?

DAVID: It's out of my hands, Ruben. [*Beat.*] You need to get to the hospital? [*Pause.*] I heard, that's all... Your aunty's been an important part of the community for a long time.

RUBEN: Yeah, well her time's pretty much up.

DAVID: I can drop you there after the session if you like? I'd like to see her actually, pay my respects.

RUBEN: It's fine.

> *Beat.*

DAVID: How is she?

RUBEN: Fine.

> *Silence.*

DAVID: I'm sorry. [*Beat.*] Hard thing, saying goodbye.

> *Beat.*

RUBEN: So what's on the cards today, Stuart Park? Let's cut the chitchat, hey. Second-to-last session. Gonna set me up with some nice little tools to guide me through the world? Give me a mantra I can whisper, help me make it through the bad times—

DAVID: Why do you do that?

RUBEN: Do what?

DAVID: Turn this into a joke.

RUBEN: [*smiling*] Coping mechanism, I guess.

DAVID: Don't be a smart-arse.

RUBEN: Well, that's what it is, isn't it? What do you want me to say?

RUBEN *laughs at himself.*

DAVID: I'm getting sick of this attitude, Ruben.

RUBEN: Is that right, Stuart Park, what you gonna / do?

DAVID: When does it end? Where does it stop? I'm obviously wasting my time here, thinkin about you, / aren't I?

RUBEN: You been thinkin about me, have ya? Naaw, I'm touched—

DAVID: Wasting my time is what it is, thinkin about you. Thinkin about how it'll end, how it turns out for you—

RUBEN: And how does it end, ay?

DAVID: Quickly. Ruben. Quickly. I blink and you're gone. You wanna muck around like this is a game? Only person who's gonna lose is you. You wanna smart-arse around like trauma's a fuckin joke? You wanna sit here and tell me about choices when week after week you come in here and deliberately dick me around, waste my time, and yours? You've had the opportunity, Ruben, the choice every week, to talk to me, to let me help you sort out the things going on in your head, but you don't wanna do that, do you? Let's be honest, you're *scared* to do that, aren't you? And like a coward you've avoided every question I've asked.

Silence.

Despite what you think, I'm not tryin to make you talk about the 'bad shit', that's not what I want. All I'm asking is for you to be honest with me. With yourself. Talk to me, none of this ego-rambling rubbish. Maybe that's what you wanna present to the world, this confident man who knows his shit, but when you don't… when you pretend with this bullshit attitude, you're not foolin' anyone. I know what it feels like, I do. You drag yourself out of a shithole, dealt a hard fuckin hand, and you've worked too long keepin your head up, I get it. Feels like all you've got are your muscles and your fists and fuck the rest, I get it, I do, but no-one's gonna hear you that way, brother, I promise you that. [*Beat.*] I'm sorry… I am. About what you and your family have been through. It shouldn't be this hard.

   Pause.

We have two more sessions as outlined by your parole officer and the DCC. I'm not signing you off after that. I'm recommending you do a further three months of counselling before your next review.

RUBEN: Are you serious?

DAVID: Do I look like I'm muckin around? [*Beat.*] What, Ruben? Really, what? You wanna ignore the hole in your chest, hug your mob after funeral time and forget about it?

   Mob can't survive like that, *you* can't survive like that. We gotta talk to each other, as hard as it is, 'cause I guarantee you, that phone will ring and you'll have to say goodbye again. [*Beat.*] You know how much we've lost. How far this thing has spread.

   Pause.

This is what we got. One shot. [*Beat.*] I'm gonna give you the option to request a new counsellor. If you'd prefer to see someone other than me, you can. We'd do the last two sessions together then if you want, we can find you someone else. I want you to know though, Rue, I want to be here. I wanna hear what you've got to say. You wanna call me Stuart Park, or dickhead, I don't care, bring it on. When the smoke's comin out your ears, or my ears, or both our ears, I wanna be here, I wanna hear it. I wanna hear you.

   Fuck sweeping it under the rug. [*Beat.*] Your move, brother.

SCENE SEVEN

Night. Rain falls softly.

Simultaneously:

RUBEN *sits under the street lamp in front of his old house. He's got a can of Southern Comfort and his earpieces in. He's singing loudly and obnoxiously as he drinks. We don't hear his music this time, just his drunk melancholic singing. He sings the first verse.*

At the same time, JARROD *and* ADELE *are at home. The mood is sombre.* JARROD *is in the kitchen looking for something to eat.* ADELE *sits at the table. They both look exhausted.*

ADELE: Jarrod, put the kettle on for us.

> JARROD *finds a biscuit tin and takes a few out. He boils the kettle.*

You pick up them magazines?

JARROD: They're in the car.

ADELE: What about that bag of clothes, the pyjamas an' that.

JARROD: In the car.

ADELE: Where the hell is this idiot now? I'm not gonna sit here, waiting for him, the fat shit. [*Beat.*] Balnba?

> *Beat.*

JARROD: After your tea, we'll go.

> *On the sidewalk under the street lamp,* RUBEN *has finished the chorus of his song, as well as his last drink. He searches around but his cans are empty. He talks to the old house.*

RUBEN: Forgot to save you some, brus. Bring you a sixer tomorrow.

> RUBEN *exits singing to himself.*

ADELE: We should pick up some flowers on the way there. The ones they sell at that poxy hospital shop are sterile.

JARROD: What, just from the servo?

> ADELE *looks at him through the back of her head. He knows she's making a face.*

What? Everywhere else is gonna be closed now, it's Tuesday, not even a bottle-o open at this hour let alone a drive-through flower shop.

ADELE: Yeh, alright. [*Beat.*] Guess I'm not thinkin straight.

JARROD: You right, bub, you don't have to, I'm 'ere.

> *The kettle boils.* JARROD *gets a cup and makes* ADELE *and himself a tea.*

I'll get some from that flower shop at Nightcliff in the morning.

> *Beat.*

ADELE: Flower shop?

JARROD: Yeah.

ADELE: Flower shop.

JARROD: Yeah, there's one at Nightcliff.

ADELE: [*smiling*] The florist…

JARROD: Yeah. At Nightcliff.

ADELE: So say it.

JARROD: Ah, Night-cliff.

ADELE: Say 'florist'.

JARROD: [*laughing*] What? Why?

ADELE: Say it, bad boy, say the word 'florist'. Say, 'I'll get some from the *florist* at Nightcliff in the morning'.

JARROD: [*laughing*] No, why? I'm too hardcore to say that word. Flower shop means the same thing, don't it?

ADELE: [*laughing*] Say it because that's what it's friggin called, it's a florist. A spade is a spade, a florist is a florist, a florist is not a flower shop. Say 'florist', ya big shit, you're not a little boy.

JARROD: Yeah, I know. [*Beat.*] Fine. I'll pick up some flowers from the florist in the morning.

> *They laugh.* JARROD *puts the tea down for* ADELE.

ADELE: You're a fuckin crack-up, boy.

JARROD: Hey, I'm a man, only mans can say words like florist. I ain't afraid of no florist.

> JARROD *sits next to* ADELE *at the table. He puts his arm around her shoulders.*

ADELE: I love you.

JARROD: I love you too, bub.

> *Pause.*

ADELE: She's gonna die, isn't she?

> *Beat.*

JARROD: Yeah.

> *Beat.*

ADELE: Tumour the size of a football, she's not even 50. It's too soon… I haven't even, she's not even a grandmother. [*Beat.*] Now I'm regretting not having a kid at 15 like the rest of Darwin. [*Beat.*] If you leave me, ever, I'll kill you, I swear to God.

JARROD: Yeah, I know.

ADELE: You don't walk out the door without comin back in, Jarrod, I'll kill you so good you'll wish you were dead.

JARROD: Not goin nowhere.

ADELE *wipes her eyes. They sit holding each other.*

Now, say my name again, I love it when you say my name.

ADELE: Shuddup, idiot—

JARROD: We can go make that grandkid now if you want?

ADELE *pushes him.*

There's a knock at the door.

I got it. I'm a man. Only mans can open doors.

JARROD *goes to the door, opens it.* PETRA *enters, wet with rain, carrying her handbag and wheeling a suitcase. In her hand she also holds some letters she's fished out of the letterbox.*

PETRA: Dry season, my arse!

JARROD: You were gonna call me, I was gonna pick you up!

PETRA *hugs* JARROD. ADELE *stands to greet* PETRA.

PETRA: I didn't fly. I drove, baby, I drove the whole damn way. You lookin solid, boy, more and more like your father every time. Help me with this bastard on wheels, would you, it won't listen to me.

JARROD *helps* PETRA *with her bag.*

ADELE: Aunty.

PETRA: Baby girl, come here, my sweets. Oh, darlin.

They hold each other.

It's alright. It's okay. You're mum's an ox. You hear me? Strongest bloody women I've ever met. Everything will be right.

She holds ADELE*'s face, looks at her.*

[*Cheerily*] You've put on weight, Del Del.

ADELE: Have I? [*Sarcastically*] Great.

PETRA: Here look, mail.

PETRA *puts the mail on the table.*

ADELE: Flick that kettle again, Jay.

PETRA: Nah, leave it, boy, it's right. Had so much caffeine on the road,

I'll be up all bloody night. What about we hit the good stuff. There's a carton in the car, Jarrod, be a love and grab it, ay.

JARROD: Rum?

PETRA: Don't go skeemin', just grab it.

> JARROD *exits to get the carton from the car.*

ADELE: I can't believe you drove.

PETRA: Was right, baby, don't you go worryin about me. Your uncle Ally didn't think I could do it, but here I am. And where's your brother now?

ADELE: I dunno, we been waiting for him for the last hour.

PETRA: Ay?

ADELE: Done this the last few times, says he's comin in with us, we're stuck here waitin and he doesn't come. End up leaving without him. [*Beat.*] He hasn't seen Mum since she went in, made every excuse. Still can't mention Joe's name around him. Every other night he's drunk in front of the old house, just drinks away his payments.

PETRA: Balnba Road?

ADELE: Just disappears, ends up there.

> *Beat.*

PETRA: Goodness. [*Beat.*] He's not as strong as you two, Del. Youse two, you got each other. [*Beat.*] We'll sort it, he'll be right. We knew early on he was gonna have it tough, no surprises there… S'pose he's always felt like a bit of a wreck, crawling out of one the way he did. [*Beat.*] You're probably too young to remember what happened on the Stuart—

ADELE: I remember.

> *Beat.*

PETRA: But I drove, baby, I drove! [*Beat.*] Enough time's passed and you start to think, 'I've got a handle on this, I know what to do with this', but it's been 15 years and still… Grief's a slippery little sucker with a mind of its own.

> PETRA *sits.*

ADELE: Probably worse for you and Mum.

PETRA: I don't think so, bub. We all have a share in it. [*Beat.*] But I finally drove. Your mother's gonna be so damn proud of me. [*Beat.*]

There's no way to avoid it, that stretch of highway. Sometimes in life you get to hide from things you don't wanna see, but there's no hidin from that accident. Even when I fly over I know exactly when I'm passin that place, can feel it in my bones. Doesn't matter if I'm asleep or nothin, I'll wake up to feel that feeling. [*Beat.*] So I called your mother this time, 'Isabel, I'm driving this time, no more planes! I'm driving'. [*Beat.*] I took the most beautiful flowers I could find in all of Alice Springs, natives of course, 'cause they last longer, and I laid them to rest right there at your aunty's cross beside that solid tree.

JARROD *returns with a carton of rum.*

Was a funeral we was drivin from… Funeral, funeral, who was it now? [*Beat.*] Ah, my uncle, your nanna's eldest brother, my second pop, beautiful man your Uncle Errol. [*To* JARROD] Well, pull 'em out, bub, no use just lookin at 'em. God, all these funerals, ay, stand like signposts, don't they?… Along the way. [*Beat.*] We was travellin in convoy, us three sisters, coming back from funeral in Alice.

JARROD *takes three cans out and distributes them. He takes a seat at the table.*

Your Aunty Lou wanted to get back quick 'cause your brother had been accepted to start school early. She thought Ruben was the smartest kid on the block. Had such high hopes, bless her… See, your brother was always tellin us these weird things. He loved science, planets and that. 'The universe, Aunty, is the biggest thing ever! Even bigger then Darwin!' Lou swore black and blue that kid would be the first blackfella in space. Hah! True God.

Beat.

Skies shoulda been clear but that year the wet broke so early we coulda swam home. Three cars, your Aunty Lou in front with Ruben. We'd stopped in Daly Waters for a feed, musta been about nine, piled all you kids back in the car, thought we'd push on another few hundred clicks—everyone seemed clear. Good.

Just before midnight it happened. Thought we'd cleared the rain but a storm front hit us hard south of Katherine. Road took us right into the belly of it. And what a belly it was. [*Beat.*] Me and Alley were number two in the convoy, and we seen something strange up ahead, a blurry little blemish between the blades of the busted wipers. And there he was, this drenched little boy, tossed about in the storm.

Beat.

I dream of him out there still, the world closing in on him. He was so terrifyingly small. High beams hit him and I thought I was dreamin. Alley lays on the brakes and sure enough, it's him, out there, in the middle of the black road. [*Beat.*] Your brother looked like a ghost, Del, if it wasn't for the blood, I would've sworn he was a ghost. [*Beat.*] We stopped. I grabbed him. Stripped him down to his gundies to check him, didn't have more then a scratch. Put him in the back seat. Your Uncle Alley followed the tracks goin off the road and Louise, my dear Lou. She wasn't wearing her belt. [*Beat.*] In my dreams it's the most peaceful thing.

Pause.

I hope she didn't wake up from that sleep. I hope that tree came and took her while she flew. That's how I like to think of it, anyway. Took her up, took her back, took her to that next place. [*Beat.*] Doesn't take much, does it. For the universe to tip on its head?

She stands, kisses ADELE*'s cheek and takes her can of rum towards the kitchen.*

It's so good to see you, my darlings, I've missed you. [*Beat.*] It'll be okay.

In the kitchen she opens the pantry cupboard, looks about.

Gotta make sure he's talking, you know? Not shrivelling up. Hopefully that counselling's doing some good.

She goes to the fridge and opens it, looks about.

Jarrod, you got credit there? Call Ruben for us, would ya? Try get this boy organised.

JARROD: No worries.

JARROD *makes the call on his mobile, stepping out of the room.*

PETRA: Any salty plums, Del? [*To* JARROD] Tell him I'm here please, son.

ADELE: That tin by the kettle.

PETRA *closes the fridge and finds the salty plum tin which she brings back to the kitchen table.* ADELE *takes one too.*

The rain outside falls heavier.

PETRA: Christ on a bike, ay, this rain! Big old low sitting right on top of us, they're sayin. Unprecedented falls… You seen it this bad before?

ADELE: No, not since—

PETRA: What?

ADELE: I said no, not since I was young!

Beat.

PETRA: First time I've done that drive by myself you know, your mum's gonna be so proud of me!

ADELE: Ay? I can't hear you!

PETRA: I said! First time I've done that drive…

PETRA *and* ADELE *yell to each other over the noise of the rain and then stop, knowing it's useless. They burst out laughing.*

They sit laughing, eating salty plums together, as the heavy rain slowly starts to subside.

It turns to light rain and JARROD *re-enters.*

ADELE: Now, what'd you say?

PETRA *cracks up laughing again.*

PETRA: Oh, my niece. Stop now, I busted my guts.

Beat.

JARROD: His phone's off, I sent him a text.

PETRA: Thank you, my boy, you're so very thorough.

ADELE: We could go past Balnba, he's probably there. [*Beat.*] Did you tell him to hurry up?

JARROD: Nah, I told him to take the long road home.

ADELE: Don't you start.

JARROD: [*cheekily*] What?

ADELE: Let's just go, ay? Stuff waitin around.

Through the screen door, RUBEN *appears.*

RUBEN: Hey, I'm here.

Beat.

JARROD: You comin in?

RUBEN: Yeah… I've got a smoke here.

ADELE: Aunty Pep's here, Rue, you're bein rude.

RUBEN: Oh shit. Aunty. Sorry.

PETRA: [*teasing*] Hurry up, boy, before I flog you.

> RUBEN *enters taking one last drag on his cigarette before he closes the door. He flicks his cigarette. He's drunk.*

RUBEN: Hey Aunty.

> *He gives* PETRA *a hug, trying to act as sober as possible.*

PETRA: Ruben Thomas Kelly, you've lost weight, ya bag of bones. Where've you been?

RUBEN: Just at Beach Front.

PETRA: You stink of grog, boy. You gonna go visit your mother like this?

RUBEN: My mother's dead.

> *Beat.*

PETRA: What did you say? [*Beat.*] Don't tell me you just said what I think you said. You wanna watch your mouth, boy, you hear me? Who do you think you're talkin to? [*Beat.*] You'd be dead too if it wasn't for my sister layin up there in that hospital. Now you have some respect and think about what you're sayin before you say it, you hear me? Don't think I'm gonna put up with your bullshit, boy. [*Beat.*] Get in the shower and wash yourself off. I don't care who you are, you're not goin to see my sister like that.

> RUBEN *starts to exit.*

Wait there.

> RUBEN *stops.*

Del, we'll go, ay. Jarrod, you can drive? You mob jump in the car.

ADELE: Grab that bag there. Jarrod.

> JARROD *grabs the bag of supplies.*

> ADELE *and* JARROD *exit.* PETRA *sits.*

PETRA: You think it's right to mess your sister round like this, you know she's been waitin for you. Not too important for you to get to the hospital, is it? Wanna piss-fart around down the pub instead? Is that even where you were? These mob aren't stupid, you know, don't think you can pull the rug. [*Pause.*] You need to take a good hard look at yourself, boy.

Who took your sorry arse in after we lost your mum. When your father took off, who took care of you then? Treated you no different then, Del, worked her arse off to put food on the table, a roof over your head, sounds like a friggin cliché, don't it, boy?—but that's what she gave you. Free a' charge.

And here we are, one time in your 21 years of livin when she needs you and you can't even stand up straight.

She waits for RUBEN *to respond. He doesn't.*

Suit yourself then, boy. You can stand there lookin at your belly button all night... better that I suppose, then come to the hospital and get on my friggin nerves. [*Beat.*] You hear what I said?

RUBEN: Yeah.

PETRA: You know why? You wanna take a guess? [*Beat.*] Izzy'd take one look at you and it'd break her heart. [*Pause.*] You know that, don't you? [*Beat.*] We'll be back in the morning. Have a shower, sleep it off.

She grabs her bag and heads for the door.

RUBEN: Aunty?

He unzips his backpack. He pulls out a bunch of frangipani stems, pulled off a tree—they're inside a plastic bag. He hasn't done it quite right but he's tried. It's beautiful.

Mum's favourite.

PETRA *takes them. She feels a little as though she's been too harsh on him. She takes the stems from the bag and wraps them in an old newspaper that's on the table.*

PETRA: Flowers, and a crossword.

She nods and smiles at her nephew.

I love you, Rue. I wouldn't say nuthin if I didn't. I'll see you tomorrow.

She exits.

As she leaves, RUBEN *notices a letter on the table. He takes it, shoves it in his backpack.*

SCENE EIGHT

DAVID *is in his office, writing at his desk. There's a knock at the door.*

DAVID: Come in.

  ADELE *enters. She stands at the door.*

ADELE: Hi, Mr Wills?

  Beat.

DAVID: Hi. Sorry, you surprised me, no-one's called me that in a while.

ADELE: Sorry.

DAVID: No no, it's fine.

ADELE: You never taught me, we never met, I just, know of you. I was in Year Eight when you left. I'm a Kelly. Adele. I'm Ruben's sister.

DAVID: Oh, hi. Of course, please, take a seat.

ADELE: Ah nah, it's okay, I'll stand.

DAVID: You sure?

ADELE: Yeah.

DAVID: Okay. [*Beat.*] So, Ruben.

ADELE: Yeah.

DAVID: He's okay, isn't he?

ADELE: Yeah, well. Yeah, just the usual. It's funny, I came here to ask you the same thing, but, um… [*Beat.*] So you work here now?

DAVID: Yeah. Been here for the last couple years.

ADELE: Didn't wanna teach anymore? [*Beat.*] Sorry… sorry, too personal. [*Beat.*] Guess we all have that in common, hey.

DAVID: What's that?

  Beat.

ADELE: Never mind. [*Beat.*] Sorry… I don't really know why I'm even here, I just thought you might… [*Beat.*] Maybe, help me.

DAVID: Sure, whatever I / can.

ADELE: Does it ever go away?

DAVID: I'm sorry?

ADELE: Does it ever go away, the picture in your head? [*Beat.*] I don't mean to be rude but, I know what happened, the whole school was talking about it. I mean, when you found him in the bathroom. The picture of him in your head, is it… is he always there? I'm prying, I know, I'm sorry, I know you're s'pose to talk about other people's problems, not your own. I know the last thing you probably need is some random askin you personal shit, but I just thought it might, help… is all. 'Cause that picture, for me, it plays over and over in this sick kind of slow motion and it's quiet but screaming all at once and I can't… I just can't get it to go. [*Beat.*] It's always with me, everywhere I go.

DAVID *steps closer to* ADELE. *She objects.*

No, it's okay, it's okay. I'm okay.

Pause.

DAVID: Maybe it never does. Go, I mean. I think it changes, I think. Somehow it becomes, bearable. [*Beat.*] He was a student of mine. For a long time I felt like I should have somehow known. I guess I've found a way to live with that, that helplessness, to live with what he left.

Beat.

ADELE: There's this spot the boys used to fish at. Jarrod, Joe and Rue. Couple of years back they rescued this tinny from the dump. It sat on the front lawn busted and full of holes so long, they nicknamed it the *Front Yard Challenge*. Eventually they patched the holes. Joey found an old motor. They'd fish all the time, the three of them. All night and all day if they could. They found this spot on the harbour with three sunken ships all in a clump. Brothers Wreck they named it, best spot on the harbour. Place is teaming with fish, get the salmon schools coming in on a high, couple of barra if you're lucky. [*Beat.*] Since Joey's gone it's like… I can't help but think we'll all end up down there, sunk. At the bottom of the ocean, clumped together. [*Pause.*] Maybe you can't talk about it, patient confidentiality or whatever, that's okay, I just… I just want to know if he's moving, not sinking, you know, I'm his big sister, it's weird for me to talk to him about this stuff. I mean I try but… I just want to know… if he's gonna be okay, I guess.

DAVID: I'm sorry, Adele, I… [*Beat.*] Ruben's missed his last two appointments. I've called and called, I've sent letters to the house, I haven't been able to get in touch with him for weeks.

ADELE: What?

DAVID: He's breached bail conditions. I'm sorry, I didn't realise you didn't know.

ADELE: Why didn't you… Fuck. [*Beat.*] I gotta go.

> ADELE *wipes her face, grabs her bag and starts to leave.*

DAVID: Adele, wait.

> ADELE *exits.*

SCENE NINE

Light rain falls.

Out the front of the old house, RUBEN *cracks another can of Southern Comfort. He is pacing back and forth. Empty cans of Southern Comfort and Coke litter the ground, some still full.*

JARROD *enters.*

JARROD: Again.

RUBEN: What?

JARROD: You, drinkin here.

RUBEN: So what?

JARROD: It's gettin weird, man, come back home, you can drink there.

RUBEN: Nah, I'm stayin here.

JARROD: Why?

RUBEN: I'm stayin.

JARROD: I heard ya, I said *why*?

> RUBEN *stops, pulls out his rollies and begins to roll.*

I'll stay too then.

RUBEN: Nah. You should go.

JARROD: I'll leave when you leave.

RUBEN: You don't have to.

> RUBEN *lights his smoke, pockets the rollies.*

JARROD: I want to. Give us a smoke, ay?

> RUBEN *fishes them from his pocket, gives one to* JARROD. *He keeps walking back and forth. Stops again, gives* JARROD *the lighter.*

RUBEN: I thought you quit.

JARROD: I'm trying to. Some days are harder then others.

RUBEN: Why bother, just smoke, Jah.

JARROD: I have to try.

RUBEN *looks at* JARROD. *They laugh.*

Shut up, I'll get it.

RUBEN: You shut up.

JARROD: No, you shut up. You're the one drinkin alone in the rain.

They smoke in silence.

RUBEN: So what does she want now?

JARROD: It's not like that.

RUBEN: What, she didn't send you?

JARROD: No, she didn't.

RUBEN: You whipped.

JARROD: Am not.

Beat.

RUBEN: What do you want?

JARROD: I just came to get you, bring you back.

RUBEN: I don't need gettin. I'll find my own way back.

JARROD: Can't a brother just hang, without the third degree?

Beat.

RUBEN: Jarrod, what do ya want?

Pause.

JARROD: She went to see your counsellor. Came back off her head. Found some letters in your room.

RUBEN: Fucken hell,

JARROD: Don't say I didn't warn ya. [*Pause.*] Oi, we should take the *Front Yard Challenge* out, Rue, I could fix her up again. The water's gone through the motor but we can fix it. It's time, don't you reckon? Run-off soon. Brothers Wreck'll be primed for a catch. Smell of salt-water got me itchin for a barra.

RUBEN: Be weird just the two of us.

JARROD: Del might wanna come.

RUBEN: I'm not fishin with dead bait.

JARROD: Oh, come on now, she's your sister.

RUBEN: You know what I'm talkin about.

JARROD: We can throw for live bait. Get another net, hit up Rapid Creek on the high, whatever. We'll find a way.

RUBEN: Just like that, ay?

JARROD: Why not?

RUBEN: Well, you can fork out the cash for it this time, I'm not payin for another one. Was brand new, 150 bucks, for fuck's sake…

Beat.

JARROD: Are you? Are you serious?

RUBEN: Leave it. I don't wanna go.

JARROD: So I'll pay for the net then.

RUBEN: I'm not goin.

JARROD: This isn't about the net.

RUBEN: Just drop it, alright?

Pause.

JARROD: Why are you here, Ruben? Of all the places you could be getting pissed you come here.

RUBEN: I wanted to be on my own, that's why I come here.

JARROD: You sure?

RUBEN: [*sarcastically*] Um, yes.

Beat.

JARROD: If this is about Joe, let's go, let's go to the cemetery. I'll come with you.

RUBEN *stops pacing.*

RUBEN: What? No, no. I don't need to. Just go. I wanna be alone.

JARROD: You're not.

RUBEN: Yeah, I can see that.

Beat.

JARROD: I'm not goin.

RUBEN: I don't need a babysitter, Jarrod, please, just fuck off. We should all just, deal with this on our own.

JARROD: Can you hear yourself?

RUBEN: I don't know, is there an echo here?

JARROD: That's more like it.

RUBEN: Please just go, dude.

JARROD: Nuh.

RUBEN: I'm serious.

JARROD: So am I. I'm not going.

RUBEN: Why can't you just, fuckin leave me alone?! I wanna be alone.

JARROD: No.

RUBEN *grabs* JARROD *by the shirt, pushing him back.*

RUBEN: Get out of here, fuck off.

JARROD: I'm not going.

RUBEN: Fuckin go. What the fuck is wrong with you?

RUBEN *pushes* JARROD *again, unable to bring himself to hit him.* JARROD *grabs onto* RUBEN *so he can't be pushed away.*

JARROD: I'm not. Going.

RUBEN: Get the fuck off me, fuck off.

JARROD: No

RUBEN: You wanna go, do ya? You wanna go down? With me, huh? You wanna go down, huh? DO YA?! Just fuck off!

JARROD *finally lets* RUBEN *go.* RUBEN *falls against the wall.*

JARROD: What'd you say that?

RUBEN: Leave me alone.

JARROD: It's not your fault.

RUBEN: I know that.

JARROD: It's not your fault.

RUBEN: I know!

Beat.

JARROD: Wouldn't have made a fuckin difference to Joe, whether you bought that throw net or not. He was reachin for something, if you hadn't of bought that net he would've found somethin else to do it with. You hear what I'm sayin? [*Beat.*] Fucken spin out, man, I don't get you, every time you two idiots were together he was the happiest I ever seen him.

RUBEN: Just fucken go!

JARROD: I'm not sayin he wasn't sick for a long time, that he didn't deserve more help then he got. I'm not saying that none of us feel like we shoulda been better friends to him, I feel that all the fucking time.

Sittin up late with him, all those nights tryin. Tryin to get through to him, talkin, always talkin, tryin to make him see something else. Trying to tell him he wasn't *alone*. Sound familiar? [*Beat.*] I know what it's like, Rue, you don't think I know? Every fuckin day I hear it— what more could I have done? Did I do enough? What if I did more? I fuckin know. And sure as I'm standin here, them thoughts will run through my head every day for the rest of my fuckin life.

RUBEN: Well, did ya, Jarrod? Did you do enough? You went to bed way early that night?! Left him with me, didn't ya?

Silence.

JARROD: I think we both did everything we coulda done. [*Beat.*] *Joey* decided he didn't wanna be here. [*Beat.*] Look at it anyway you fuckin like, but you stop right fuckin now, takin credit for something you never done.

Silence.

I'm not leaving till you're leaving.

Beat.

RUBEN: Then I guess we're fuckin leaving then.

RUBEN exits. JARROD follows.

SCENE TEN

Back at home, ADELE *is sitting at the table with three letters that she's opened.* PETRA *is sitting next to her.*

RUBEN *enters, followed by* JARROD.

ADELE: What are these? [*Beat.*] What the hell are these?

She throws the letters at RUBEN. *She keeps one in her hand, holding it high above her head. She recites words she's memorised.*

'In accordance with the Prisons Correctional Services Act, please be advised that your parole has been revoked.'

ADELE *chucks the piece of paper.*

RUBEN: I know what it says, Del. You went into my room?

ADELE: You think I wouldn't find out? You think I wouldn't put two and two together when you got arrested?

RUBEN: You should mind your own business, that's what you should fuckin do—

ADELE: You are my business, dickhead, if something happens to you, I am. I am. I am...

JARROD: Babe—

ADELE: You stay the fuck out of it.

RUBEN: I've seen him once a week for the last three months, alright? He's makin me go another three and I won't do it.

ADELE: You got it all sorted, have ya?

RUBEN: Del.

ADELE: Have ya?

RUBEN: I'm sick of fuckin talkin about it!

ADELE: So you wanna get locked up then, is that it?

RUBEN: No.

ADELE: So what are you doing? [*Beat.*] What the fuck are you doing then?! They will lock you up, Rue, they will lock you up and no-one can help you once you're in there—do you get that? Do you understand that, egghead? And what do I do when you're in there? What the fuck do I do? Did you even think about what happens to the rest of us while you're in there? Big fuckin protector of the family. And what about Mum? Ay? 'Sorry, Mum, I know you're really sick and all, but Ruben's having trouble coming anywhere near the hospital. *PLUS*. He's in *lockup*.' Is that what I tell her? [*Beat.*] Fuckin answer me, Ruben, is that what I / tell her?

RUBEN: I can't watch anyone else die!

Silence.

ADELE: Yeah, well. Neither can I.

Pause.

PETRA: Sit down please, Ruben.

RUBEN: Nah, fuck this.

PETRA: I said sit the fuck down!

RUBEN: Why?! I don't need this, I don't need another fuckin lecture 'bout how to live my life. If youse don't like what I'm doin then youse can fuck off! This is bullshit— [*To* ADELE] I don't go behind your back snooping for shit! [*Beat.*] I'm fuckin outta here.

RUBEN *exits. He heads to his room to pack a bag.*

JARROD, ADELE *and* PETRA *are left in the room, waiting.*

ADELE *paces.*

ADELE: [*yelling to* RUBEN *offstage*] She's asking for you, Mum is! [*Beat.*] She knows what's goin on, fuck knows why she keeps askin but she's asking for you! We're running out of lies!

PETRA: It's okay, bub.

ADELE: He's got nowhere to go.

PETRA: He's angry, he'll calm down.

RUBEN *re-enters carrying a duffle bag filled with clothes spilling out of it.*

Sit down please, son.

RUBEN: I'm not your fuckin son.

JARROD: [*to* RUBEN] Oi!

PETRA *approaches* RUBEN, *puts her hand on his chest.*

PETRA: [*calmly*] Hey, I know you're upset, but what did I say about the way you speak to me? Look at me, son. [*Beat.*] Come on. You look at me.

RUBEN *looks at her.*

What do you see? What do you see? [*Beat.*] I am my sister. And she is me. Me and your mother we got the one blood. You sabi? You understand, Rue? [*Beat.*] I asked you before, please, sit down. You wanna go after that, you can go.

RUBEN *begrudgingly sits.* PETRA *takes a seat beside him.*

Now there's a warrant for your arrest, bub, so first things first, let's give your counsellor a call and make you an appointment. Then we can call the police and—

RUBEN: What? No, I just said, I'm not going back to / see that maggot, he's a dog—

ADELE: He's been through the / same thing we have!

RUBEN: I'm not going back to / him!

PETRA: If one of the neighbours calls the police 'cause we're all fuckin yellin at each other! *You're* the first one they're gonna lock up, Rue, is that what you want? [*Beat.*] Right, so get on the phone and call David, somebody.

ADELE *gets her phone out and finds the piece of paper with David's number on it.*

RUBEN: I'm not talkin to him.

PETRA: Then who you gonna talk to? Me? Your sister? Jarrod? They been tryin to talk to you for months, and what? Instead you end up with a gut full of piss out front of a house full of ghosts. I don't want you going to jail… let's just give him a call / and—

RUBEN: I'm out.

PETRA: Ruben!

As RUBEN *gets up to grab his bag of packed clothes,* JARROD *follows, quickly grabbing him by the scruff of his neck, pushing him up against the nearest wall.*

JARROD: You're not the only one who lost him.

Beat.

RUBEN: Get off me.

JARROD *lets* RUBEN *go.*

RUBEN *exits.*

SCENE ELEVEN

Rain falls steadily outside the old house that Jarrod, Adele, Ruben and Joe lived in.

RUBEN *is breaking in through a window. He takes louvres out, one at a time. The room is completely empty, no curtains on the windows, the air is damp and musty. Occasionally headlights pass by, lighting the room, otherwise it's quite dark.*

Before climbing through the window RUBEN *drops in a sixpack of rum and a fresh pack of smokes. As he climbs through, one of his arms gets caught on some metal. It starts bleeding immediately. He falls into the room bleeding and swearing.*

RUBEN: Fuck. Fuck. Muthafucka!

Completely overcome with frustration he peels cans of rum from the sixer and smashes them against the wall one after the other, swearing, until he only has a few left.

Fuck. Fuck you. Fuck you!

He falls to the floor, exhausted and wrecked. He uses his shirt to stop the bleeding. As tears rush down his face, he wipes them away.

I wanted to learn how to throw, remember? I woulda been happy to just keep chuckin the bastard till I knocked the fish out, but I knew I could learn. I wanted to do something good. I wanted us to be the best fishermen the harbour had ever seen, I wanted to live like my grandfathers lived, I wanted to know what it felt like to be proud of myself. So I bought the net. I bought the net. [*Beat.*] We drank in the driveway till four, it was about four I think, I fell asleep in the chair. I woke up 'cause, 'cause you changed the music. I yelled at you to turn it down. I think it was four. [*Beat.*] I came inside, I felt sick. I had to sleep. I, I crashed on the couch. [*Beat.*] I was gone, out of it, till you shook me. You shook me awake. 'Ruben, wake up, man, come look at this.' [*Beat.*] I was heavy, I couldn't, I couldn't. [*Beat.*] 'Fuck off, Joe, I've had enough, let me sleep.' [*Beat.*] 'Let me sleep,' I said.

Pause.

You let me sleep. [*Beat.*] I woke. I thought I heard mice, scampering, scratching, frantic. [*Beat.*] Then it stopped.

Pause.

I lay awake, wondering what it was. By the time I got outside it was too late. You'd stopped moving. I saw the net, the sinkers scraping, all wrapped around, your feet just touching the bottom of the pipe. It wasn't mice, it was you. [*Beat.*] Lift him up! Lift him up! Lift him up! [*Beat.*] Too late. [*Beat.*] You're gone. [*Beat.*] I should've got up. You asked me to get up. Fuck! Why didn't I get up?!

Pause.

No matter what, you always had time for me. No matter what, you were always there for me. [*Beat.*] I won't ever be the same, Joe. I…

Pause.

I sat there. I couldn't move. [*He can't help but cry.*] I tried to tell Del, I did, when she woke up I tried to say something before she saw you, nothing came out. I was stuck, and they found you and I couldn't move, I couldn't move, I don't know what happened, I couldn't move. I'm so sorry, I should've got up, I should've helped get you down, I was stuck. I couldn't move! That whole time I couldn't move, I tried, I did, that whole day I prayed that I'd move, please let me fucking move!

Suddenly torchlight is seen through the windows, sweeping the room, searching for something.

The door opens. ADELE, JARROD, PETRA *and* DAVID *enter.*

RUBEN *stands, confronts them. He's completely unsure of where he is and what is happening.*

Where the fuck have you cop cunts been? Fucking useless pigs! / You'll rot in hell for this, you dogs!

ADELE: Hey hey, / hey hey, woah, Ruben!

RUBEN: You cunts / can't get anything fuckin right, can ya?

PETRA: Ruben, hey / hey, HEY!

JARROD: Oi, Ruben!

RUBEN *launches himself at them.* ADELE *and* PETRA *scramble backwards.* JARROD *and* DAVID *quickly move forward and try to restrain him.* RUBEN *lands a punch on* DAVID*'s jaw,* DAVID *doesn't miss a beat.*

RUBEN: Where the fuck have you been? We can't cut him down! Joey's been out there all day! Where have you been? Don't leave him out there, cut him down now! He's been there all fuckin day! THE WHOLE DAY HE'S BEEN THERE! Where the fuck have you been?! / Cut him down, cut him down, please cut him down! Please!

DAVID: Ruben. Ruben. Ruben. Ruben, it's me David, it's David, Ruben. Look at me, Ruben, it's me David. / Ruben, Ruben, Ruben, it's okay, mate, everything's okay.

JARROD *and* DAVID *manage to get* RUBEN *to the ground. He is completely broken.*

RUBEN: Cut him down, cut him down, cut him down, cut him down, / cut him down, cut him down, cut him down please, cut him down…

JARROD: It's okay, Rubes, it's okay. It's okay he's down, brother, we got him down.

Lights out.

SCENE TWELVE

Music plays.

ADELE, JARROD *and* PETRA *are sitting at the kitchen table. They have cups of tea.*

ADELE: I'm exhausted.

PETRA: Wish I could tell you it gets easier, bub.

> *Pause.*

ADELE: Aunty? I'm sorry I walked out today when Mum was talking about the funeral. [*She laughs.*] I started crying and I couldn't stop, I just wanted to stop and keep it together, but I couldn't. I didn't want Mum to think it was upsetting me 'cause I know she needed to tell us how she wants things to be, I just couldn't…

PETRA: Del, it's fine, bub, don't / worry.

ADELE: I just couldn't be in that room. I heard what she said, I did, I just sat outside the door, I heard it all. Pink at the funeral, no-one in black. Frangipanis and balloons, I wrote it all down.

PETRA: We knew you were still there at the door, Del. [*Beat.*] What'd ya think, we were laughin?

ADELE: Great.

PETRA: We had a good little chuckle, Del, I was makin hand signals, ya mum shh-ing me to stop. [*Beat.*] We weren't laughin *at* ya, Del… [*Beat.*] Your mother, since you was a little girl, used to call me up every other week talkin about your little menagerie at home, nursing birds back to good health, the frogs, the lizards, the rabbit you saved from the python at Palmerston—God, I seem to recall her saying you made her feed a cockroach in a jar for days after you found him with a busted leg. [*Beat.*] She knows you, bub, she loves that about you. That you aren't afraid to feel. [*Beat.*] Just like your Nanna June you are, cryin when she was happy, and cryin when she was sad. Only way to get through this world, Del, let it all hang out. Don't you ever apologise for that.

> JARROD *is smiling. He reaches for* ADELE*'s hand across the table.*

And what you smiling for, handsome?

JARROD: Nothin, Aunty, it's just really good to have you here.

PETRA: Well, youse might as well get used to it. Looks like I'll be stickin around for a while... Youse mob can't be runnin around here, free-range.

ADELE: Jesus, Jarrod, your hands are filthy. Can't you wipe them first before you get grease all over the table?

JARROD: Oh, come oooon, I was gettin happy to hold your hand.

> ADELE *goes to wash her hands while* JARROD *cleans his greasy hands on his greasy shirt.*

PETRA: How's that motor comin along, boy, how long till she's back in the water?

JARROD: She's seaworthy as we speak, Aunty, took her for a float this arvo, she's purring like a cat.

PETRA: That's my boy, you told Ruben?

> RUBEN *enters.*

RUBEN: Told Ruben what?

JARROD: The *Front Yard Challenge*, she sails again, bro.

RUBEN: Oh, the tinny sails, ay?

JARROD: Don't be stupid, you know what I mean.

RUBEN: You took her out?

JARROD: Just Rapid Creek. We could take her out for a sneaky creek run before the arvo storm one morning if you're keen?

> *Pause.*

ADELE: How's David doin?

RUBEN: He's good.

ADELE: Should I give him a call?

RUBEN: You can if you want, stickybeak, he said he's droppin by later in the week.

PETRA: I should hope so, he's promised your mother more of them salty plums he gave us, God knows how, but she's run out. Buggered if I know where she's puttin them, I'm sure she had half a bag yesterday and now, they're suddenly gone! [*Beat.*] You can never keep a Darwin girl from her salty plums, I'll tell ya that right now.

RUBEN: How is Mum?

PETRA: She's doing alright today, bub, holding on.

She stands, collects her teacup and heads for the sink.

Now who's comin with me? We best collect a few things and chuck on some washing before we head back to the hospital—I'm gettin stinkin in these clothes and it's gettin late.

RUBEN: Aunty…

PETRA: It's okay, lovie, I told Mum / it might be some time before you—

RUBEN: I wanna come. [*Beat.*] I wanna come. With you. To the hospital.

Pause.

PETRA: Okay, bub. [*Beat.*] Okay. [*Pause.*] Alright, ya stunned mullets, come on then, let's move, ay, grab ya things, I'll chuck the washing on, rinse your cups please. All the stinkin mugs are disappearing so check the bedrooms if you will, I'll run the water. Make me weak, youse mob, true God in heaven, today.

ADELE *and* JARROD *exit.*

RUBEN *collects the dishes he can see, takes them to the sink.* PETRA *comes to him, she touches his head.*

Hey. [*Beat.*] Your mother would be so proud of you, boy. And me and your other mother, we proud as punch too.

They stand together. RUBEN *stops washing and it's quiet for a moment. Then* PETRA *gives him a nudge.*

Ay, I didn't say stop washing now.

PETRA *grabs his head and kisses him on the cheek as he starts doing the dishes again.*

THE END